IN MY PAIN I FOUND MY PURPOSE
By Sharon McKinney

Table of Contents
Foreword by Dr. Tamia Dow
A Letter of Gratitude
Chapter 1 – The Beginning of How the Journey Began
Chapter 2 – The Teen Crying Out
Chapter 3 – Slowly Losing Myself
Chapter 4 – Hiding Behind the Pain
Chapter 5 – Lost and Without Hope
Chapter 6 – Light at the End of the Tunnel
Chapter 7 – Surrendering
Chapter 8 – Grief and Loss
Chapter 9 – Just Existing but Not Really Living
Chapter 10 – Finding My Purpose

Foreword

by Dr. Tamia Dow

There are moments in life that only God can orchestrate — moments where pain and purpose collide, and something beautiful is born. One of those moments for me was the day I met Sharon McKinney.

I was a police officer in Las Vegas, and she was working the streets, surviving the only way she knew how. The world saw her as broken and unworthy. But I saw something different — I saw a woman that God loved deeply, a woman He had a plan for. I remember telling her, "You don't belong out here. God has more for your life."

At that time, I had no idea how those words would one day come full circle. I never imagined that years later, Sharon and I would be serving side by side — two women who had once been on opposite sides of the same battle — now united in Christ, ministering to survivors of domestic violence and sex trafficking.

Sharon's journey is nothing short of miraculous. She overcame addiction, abuse, and the crushing grief of losing her son. She endured physical pain and yet, even from her hospital bed, she prayed for others. Her faith never quit. Her heart never stopped believing that God would use her story to help others find hope.

This book, "In My Pain I Found My Purpose," is more than testimony — it is transformation. It's a story of a woman who refused to give up, who found the love of God when the world gave her none, and who now shines as a beacon of hope for others. I am so proud of the woman Sharon has become — strong, compassionate, and full of the Spirit of God. Her life reminds us that no matter where we've been, God can redeem it all. He can take what was meant for harm and turn it into healing for others.

It is my honor to write this foreword for my sister, Chaplain Sharon McKinney — proof that pain can birth purpose, and that God's love truly changes everything.

Award Winning and Best Selling Author
Dr. Tamia Dow
Retired Police Officer
Pastor • Chaplain • Founder, Dr. Tamia Dow Ministries
Las Vegas, Nevada

A Letter of Gratitude
To My Husband and My Daughter,
Thank you.
From the depths of my heart, thank you for loving me, supporting me, and standing beside me through every step of this journey. Writing this book has been one of the most meaningful and transformative experiences of my life, and I could not have done it without you both. Thank you for giving me the time, the space, and the grace to pour my heart onto these pages. Thank you for understanding the late nights, the early mornings, and the moments when my mind was wrapped in thoughts and words. Your patience and your unwavering belief in me gave me the strength to keep going, even on the days when I questioned myself.
To my husband—your love has been my anchor. Your encouragement has been my fuel. Thank you for covering me, uplifting me, and reminding me that my voice matters.
To my daughter—you inspire me more than you will ever know. Thank you for your hugs, your smiles, and your gentle reminders that I can do hard things. You are one of the greatest reasons I push forward with purpose.
This book is not just my accomplishment—it is ours.
Thank you for being my strength, my peace, and my motivation.
With all my love,
Sharon Mckinney

And to everyone who has supported me along this journey—your prayers, your words, your presence, and your belief in this vision have meant more than you could ever imagine. I am truly grateful for every single one of you.

Steven Deutsch

Bart and Janice

Jason and Jessica

CHAPLAIN Dow

Rachel Richardson

Jon Ponder

Victoria From Chaplaincy Nevada

Bishop Naida Parson

Pastor Tiffany Trass

Jennifer

Amina and Anthony Forte

Cedric Shelby

Regina Rhodes

Leona Huntertle

I love each and every one of you.

Sharon Mckinney

Chapter 1
The Beginning of How the Journey Began

From the very beginning, my story was layered with identity, confusion, culture, and pain. I was born into an Orthodox Jewish family, connected to the tribe of Levi—the tribe of Moses. Yet despite that strong lineage, I grew up feeling disconnected, unseen, and longing for something I could not name at the time.

My earliest memory of my father is a strange one—him carrying my mother over his shoulders. As a child, I didn't understand what I was seeing. Years later, when I asked my mother about it, she told me he had been taking her into another room to beat her because she wouldn't let him abuse me in front of her. The screaming I heard… the crying I tried to interpret as laughter… those were the sounds of violence. That memory was all I had of him.

Everything else was silence.

Despite this, my early childhood had moments of innocence. I grew up believing in Santa Claus, celebrating Christmas, and enjoying big family gatherings—though these things didn't line up with my Orthodox Jewish upbringing. We had Christmas trees, lights, stockings, and presents—yet we also kept Jewish traditions: Passover dinners, Yom Kippur, Rosh Hashanah, and eventually, my Bat Mitzvah at fifteen. These mixed traditions created a confusion in me that followed me through childhood.

Later, we moved to a house in Summerdale, New Jersey. That's where kindergarten started for me. I remember the snow falling outside, the little heater inside the school where we warmed our gloves, and the joy of making snow angels. I remember licking icicles off the roof, riding my tricycle, and making my first friends: a girl whose backyard connected to ours, another who lived across the street, and even my sister's pet goose, who became my playmate before I had real friends of my own. Because I had no relationship with my own father, I longed desperately for one. When I saw my friend's father loving his children, playing with them, talking to them—I asked her if he could be my dad, too. I just wanted someone who would care for me the way I saw him caring for his own.

At home, things were different. My mother had a boyfriend, my sister had hers, and our basement was always full of people. My mom managed a band, so musicians were constantly coming in and out of the house. Cigarette smoke, loud voices, and the smell of alcohol became normal. I rode my tricycle up and down the street, the wheels squeaking because my mom refused to oil them—she wanted to know how far I'd gone by the sound.
I remember birthday parties in the backyard with barbecues and grown-ups everywhere, and a man who showed up with a motorcycle giving kids rides. Those were the lighter moments. But the contradiction in my household always lingered—Jewish roots mixed with Christmas celebrations, structure mixed with chaos, culture mixed with trauma.

As I grew older, I began attending Jewish camps, learning Hebrew prayers, and participating in the rituals of my heritage. In school, though, my world expanded beyond my Jewish identity. I found myself drawn into African American communities and culture. The street we lived on was all Caucasian families, but just up the hill was a predominantly African American neighborhood. Even as a child, I sensed the quiet segregation.

My mother, my sister, and I would sometimes drive through the African American neighborhood, windows down, catching the smell of barbecue filling the air. The aroma was sweet, smoky, unforgettable—like the whole block was alive. I didn't know why we drove through there so often... whether it was curiosity, comfort, or a silent longing for community. But those moments stayed with me.

These memories are resurfacing now as I share my testimony—things I buried for years under layers of pain.

Because underneath the laughter, the friends, the holidays, and the summer memories...

I was a little girl who felt unwanted.

A little girl who believed her father didn't love her.

A little girl who once told her mother, "I wish I had never been born."

My mother told me, "Your father wanted you. He even named you before you were born."

But that only made the pain sharper. If he wanted me so badly, why wasn't he there? What did I do wrong? Was I ugly? Was I too skinny? Why did he choose to leave?

Those questions became wounds.

My siblings were much older—my sister ten years older and my brother five. My sister often cared for me. She crocheted Barbie clothes, painted my nails, cooked for me, and taught me girly things. My brother defended me, sometimes taking the blame for things I had done. I was close to them… but it didn't replace the emptiness of not having my father.

Meanwhile, the adults in our house created an unsafe environment. My mother's boyfriend was abusive—not only to her, but toward me in ways that left lifelong scars. I told my mother he touched me. She said it was just a nightmare. When it happened again, I described every detail, but her response was still small, still dismissive, still "What happens in this house stays in this house."

I carried that secrecy like a chain.

The man eventually became violent toward my mother—throwing her off the porch and breaking her arm. I feared him. I feared the chaos. And I feared what life might've been like if my father had stayed… would things have been different?

One Christmas Eve, I waited for my father to pick me up. My mother had wrapped a tie for him. I fell asleep waiting. He never came. He never called. That memory became another scar.

School was my escape—my safe place. Field trips to New York, Philadelphia, the Mint, the Statue of Liberty… those moments gave me joy. My friends gave me joy. Their families gave me glimpses of the stability I longed for. At some homes we prayed before dinner—something foreign to me even though I grew up in a religious household. But their prayers were different. They prayed to God, not just in tradition.

I loved being with friends because their homes felt like what a family should be.

Back home, I was exposed to things no child should see—drinking, drugs, men coming and going, music blasting, and an atmosphere where anything could happen. I started smoking cigarettes young, hiding them in my sock, pretending to be older than I was. I learned how to sneak beer and weed. My mother would say, "If you're going to smoke, smoke here so I can see you." That was the environment I was raised in.

Still, God gave me friendships that lasted a lifetime. Some of those friends are still in my life today. They watched me walk through storms, heartbreaks, losses, and transitions. Even without using names, they know who they are. They were part of the good in my childhood.

As elementary school ended, I transitioned into junior high, carrying both my memories and my wounds with me—still searching for love, still searching for acceptance, still searching for the father I never had, and still trying to make sense of the world I had been born into.
This was the beginning of my journey.

Chapter 2
The Teen Crying Out

I was twelve years old—still a child, but already carrying the weight of an adult—when I boarded that plane alone from Philadelphia to California. My brother and sister dropped me off at the airport, and before I knew it, I was in the air, heading into a life I didn't understand. I remember the layover in Dallas, getting off one plane and onto another by myself. I didn't know where I was going, who I was going to, or what waited for me on the other side. I just remember the fear of being alone in the sky.

When the plane landed, a stewardess walked me off and handed me over to my mother—who wasn't alone. Her boyfriend stood beside her, waiting. My heart dropped. I was already angry, hurt, and confused, and having him there made everything worse. All I had was my small suitcase and a big black trash bag filled with Tupperware she had asked me to bring. That was my introduction to California.

We went to his apartment—an apartment meant for singles—which is where we stayed for two days. Then my mother made arrangements for me to stay with the woman selling them a house. A complete stranger. I was to live at her place during the week—twenty minutes from my mother—because her daughter went to a different school. I had to ride my bike nearly thirty minutes to the junior high where they decided I should attend, starting my eighth-grade year all over again, making new friends all over again, starting my life all over again.

That became my routine—weekdays with the realtor's family in Lakewood, weekends with my mom and her boyfriend in Long Beach, and school in Bellflower. Three cities. One girl. No stability.

On weekends, they dragged me along to places I never asked to go—Malibu, San Diego, SeaWorld, Disneyland, Grauman's Chinese Theater, the Wax Museum. Places I would have loved to go with just my mom, but instead I was forced to third-wheel their attempts at forming a "family." They planned everything without asking my feelings, my thoughts, my wants. I wasn't included in decisions, only expected to follow.

Inside, the walls I had already built began rising higher. I felt invisible, voiceless, and powerless. They said they were doing all these things for me, but it never felt that way. It felt like they were doing it for themselves—trying to force a family image that my heart rejected.

I never saw him as a father and refused to. Yet they tried to push that relationship on me. He once took me out alone—I think to a mall, maybe Chick-fil-A or Orange Julius. I didn't want to eat; I didn't even want to be there. He sat there eating, trying to talk, telling me to grab food to take home. But no one had asked if I wanted to go. It was all forced.

During that conversation, he told me he was going to be in my life because he was with my mother. He said he wanted to build a relationship with me. I just stared, silent, angry, violated. I felt like my feelings should have mattered, that I should have had a say in who had access to my life. And knowing the abuse he inflicted on my mom only made me reject the idea even more.

Then he said he wanted to become a Jew. I didn't care. I wasn't impressed. I figured he was doing it for my mother or for the "family image" he wanted to create.

And so began the temple visits. They found a rabbi, went to counseling, and dragged me along to children's programs. Soon, summer arrived and I was sent to a full Jewish camp, learning the Torah, the laws, and traditions at a level I never had back east. I should have been preparing for ninth grade, moving into our house in Bellflower, but the house wasn't ready yet, so everything remained in limbo.

Eventually my Bat Mitzvah came—planned entirely by them. None of my family from back east came. Not one. It was just my mom, her boyfriend, and me. I told myself at least I was around other kids, hoping maybe someone from the Jewish camps would be there.

School, though, was another trauma. I didn't care about learning—I was too busy trying to survive emotionally. I was trying to find friends, trying to find myself, trying to understand who I was, while still thinking constantly about my father.

Adjusting to California was a battle. I had to change the way I dressed because east coast fashion didn't fit in on the west coast.

Dolphin shorts instead of gauchos, different shoes, different everything. Kids laughed at my long New Jersey accent. When I was asked to read out loud, I could hear the snickers behind me. I told the teacher I didn't want to read, but she made me anyway.

I felt like an outsider in every room I entered.

I missed my cousins, my grandmother, the basements we played in, the sleepovers, the dolls, the laughter, the familiarity. Now everything was single-story houses, new faces, and no sense of belonging. It felt like losing a part of myself.

My sister came to visit once with her little girl. I adored that baby. She was my little live Barbie doll, my joy, my escape. I would lay her on a pillow and fly her around like she was on a magic carpet. That memory still warms me.

But soon they left too. I still don't know the details of why. My brother wasn't there yet either. So much of that time is a blur because I blocked out the hurt, the confusion, the unanswered questions.

Looking back now, I know I wasn't just running from the pain—I was running from my purpose, my calling, and even from who I was becoming. I was running from my old self while desperately trying to find my new one. The hardest part was having so many questions and no one to ask. Too many years had passed, too many memories buried, too much pretending that none of it happened. I ran away from home more times than I can count—trying to escape something I didn't have the words for. Trying to save a little girl inside me who was crying out, hoping someone would finally hear her.

.

Chapter 3
Slowly Losing Myself

By ninth grade, life looked different on the outside, but inside I was slowly falling apart. I had started high school, made new friends—kids who lived right down the street and some I had known since first moving into the neighborhood. We went to house parties, and I drank here and there. I had stopped smoking marijuana, but only because the man who once lived in our house—the one whose presence made being sober unbearable—was finally gone. Looking back now, that speaks volumes. I didn't want to be home unless I was numbed. Being sober meant feeling everything I was desperate to escape. Marijuana had become my pain reliever, my silencer, my way of covering my cries when no one else could hear them.

Earlier in my story, I mentioned trying mushrooms and LSD. The truth is, I never willingly tried them. I didn't know the marijuana I smoked was dipped in it until after it hit me. That high was nothing like the numbness I was used to. Instead of feeling calm, I panicked. I became paranoid—feeling watched, followed, unsafe. My vision doubled and tripled. Pictures blurred and intertwined. It was a frightening, anxious hallucination that I didn't have the language to describe back then. After that experience, I stopped smoking altogether.

For a moment, life seemed like it might settle into something "normal." My sister, her boyfriend, and my niece moved into our house temporarily before getting their own place in Lakewood. But the man she was with—the same boyfriend she had back in New Jersey—the same man who used to come into my room, pull up a chair, sit there, stare at me, and touch me in ways he never should have… he was back in my life again.

I remember avoiding him at all costs. My mom was gone a lot, my sister was gone sometimes, and I never knew who was supposed to be watching the house—or watching me. He would listen at my door. He would try to look through my window. I never wanted to be in the same room with him. Even as an adult, I avoided family gatherings if he was attending. Even when I got married, I refused to show up to events where he would be.

It wasn't fear—at least not the kind you can name. It was a deep ache. A wound. A reminder of everything I didn't want to feel.

My mother's boyfriend and my sister's boyfriend had both violated my safety in different ways, and that pain shaped my understanding of "family." I was living inside dysfunction, and I didn't know any other way to exist.

Talking about this part of my life is still painful, but necessary. That trauma shaped so much of my adolescence. It robbed me of the childhood I should have had. And it wasn't my fault. It wasn't my mother's fault. It wasn't my sister's fault. It was just the brokenness of that time. This was 1979—before electronics, before distraction, before any real escape except the ones you had to create for yourself.

By then, I had fallen in with the stoners and surfers—kids who were hurting just like me. We got high, drank, ditched school. I became good at knowing exactly which classes I could skip without my mother noticing. I didn't miss enough to fail completely—just enough to breathe. I even tried to change an F to a B on my report card once. Those old-school printed cards didn't budge. I learned the hard way.

Around this time, my mother's boyfriend was officially gone, my sister moved out, my brother moved in, and I began asking questions about my father.

"Mom, why do my brother and sister have their father, but I don't have mine?"

That's when she finally told me her version of what happened—that she came home one day to find a "For Sale" sign in the yard, and my father had supposedly run off with a neighbor. I asked why he left. She didn't know, or said she didn't. I asked if she could help me find him so I could write him. She claimed she tried, but letters were returned. Sometimes I wonder if she really did.

Later in life, I learned even more secrets—truths that only added salt to old wounds—but that comes later in this story.

In high school, I wasn't into sports or clubs. My escape was hanging out with friends. Anything to be outside the house. Anything to avoid the pain inside. Eventually, everything built up so heavily that I ran away. I ended up in juvenile hall. The police found marijuana in my car, but they didn't charge me. In the late '70s, it was nothing more than a slap on the wrist.

But my running wasn't rebellion—it was desperation. I was trying to disappear.

One day I drove my little Datsun B210 into the mountains—the same area where I had once been sent to Jewish camp. I planned never to return home. It started snowing, and I stopped at a small café decorated with Christmas lights. I was freezing, wearing no jacket, no extra clothes. When the waitress asked if I was okay, I told her, "No. I'm running away."

She brought me something warm to eat. But before I could take a bite, a police officer came in and asked, "Are you Sharon?" That was the end of my escape.

In juvenile hall, I refused to eat. My mother tried visiting. I refused to come out. I felt numb—tired of running, tired of hurting. But since they had no charges to hold me on, they released me back to my mother. The car ride home was silent until she stopped and asked if I wanted Taco Bell. I ate, but I didn't feel connected to myself. I told her I wasn't happy. She asked if I wanted counseling. I told her no. I didn't trust anyone enough to say yes.

My mother was working for a major law firm at that time—the same one that helped bring the Oakland Raiders to Los Angeles. She would get free tickets to games and concerts like the Rolling Stones and Prince. She took me often, sometimes forcing me to go just to keep tabs on me. She even sent my younger niece to "babysit" me—though as adults, we later learned she was really sent to watch over me.

Despite everything happening around me, she became one of my closest companions. My niece became the one person who unknowingly helped me hold it together.

Still, the restlessness inside me didn't go away. I tried running away again. This time neighbors were watching me. My mother had basically appointed them as spies.

They would call her with every move I made. I felt suffocated, exposed, and embarrassed.

By the time I graduated, I was already losing pieces of myself. And then, right out of high school, I met the man who would become my children's father. We went horseback riding, and before long, we were living in his parents' garage. At 19 years old, I called my mother and told her casually, "By the way, I'm married. And I'm pregnant."

That pregnancy ended in a miscarriage at six months. Losing a child while feeling the kicks, hearing the heartbeat, and imagining the future felt like losing a part of my soul. First the forced abortion I never wanted. Then a miscarriage. Two pieces of me gone before I ever got to hold them.

I named my baby boy Jason—Joshua in Hebrew—meaning "healer and deliverer." I didn't know that until years later. Maybe God named him. Maybe God knew how deeply I needed healing.

Life moved forward. I became a directory assistance operator—411. I always added a little blessing to the end of each call, something small to show kindness in the world.

Eventually, I became pregnant again, this time with my daughter. My miracle baby. My gift. She arrived by emergency C-section in 1987, but she was beautiful, perfect, and exactly what my heart had been waiting for. The son I lost had been my promise, but my daughter felt like God's reminder that I was still worthy of joy.

My marriage wasn't easy. There was drinking. Arguments. Abuse. Nights where he stayed out late at bars. But I held onto the relationship because I wanted my children to grow up with both parents under the same roof. Even when it hurt. Even when I felt alone. During the Whittier earthquake, I was on the second floor, terrified, holding my children close. And that moment—like so many others—reminded me that I had learned to survive chaos from a young age. Survival had become my normal.

I didn't know it then, but slowly, through all of this, I was losing myself piece by piece.

Chapter 4
Hiding Behind the Pain

I had a son—Jason. At the time, I didn't know that his name meant healer in Hebrew. I didn't know it meant deliverer. I only discovered this years later, when I finally sat down to write this book—the same book God told me long ago to write, but I wasn't ready for the process then. God had to take me through the journey first. Through the depression of losing my first child to abortion. Through the heartbreak of miscarriage. Through the wounds of abuse—mental and physical—that still lived inside me. Maybe that is why God placed the name "Jason" in my heart. Maybe He named my son Himself.

Life went on. We were living in a new house, and once Jason was old enough to stay with a babysitter, I got a job. Soon after, I landed a different position as a directory assistance operator—411 dispatch. When callers phoned in, I would say, "What city, please?" Then, before hanging up, I always added something extra: "Have a blessed day," or "Thank you for calling—God bless you."
A small seed of kindness I planted each day, even though I was still lost.
Not long after starting that job, I became pregnant again—this time with my daughter. She was born in 1987 by emergency C-section. It had been a good year and a half, maybe two, between the children.
By the time I conceived her, we were living in an upstairs three-bedroom apartment.

At the doctor's appointment right before her birth, they discovered she was breech.

"If she doesn't turn, we'll take her by C-section," the doctor said. We went home, preparing to barbecue with friends, when suddenly —I went into labor. My water broke on the way to the hospital.

I called the doctor before we left, and he told us to go straight to labor and delivery, where he would meet us. When we arrived, the nurse checked me and realized the baby was coming—and she was still breech.

And then she was here.

Beautiful. My angel. My gift from God.

Jason was God's promise, but Jessica felt like the frosting on the cake. Both my children are miracles to me, but my daughter… she was the longing of my heart fulfilled. In my first pregnancy, I wanted a baby girl so badly. I was disappointed when I learned I was having a boy—though their father was thrilled. When Jessica arrived, it felt like heaven had whispered a second chance.

Even with the joy of our children, our relationship continued its cycle of ups and downs. I was determined to keep our marriage together, no matter what. I wanted my children raised with both parents in the home—even though that home was filled with dysfunction. Yes, there was still abuse. He continued drinking, staying out late at bars with friends or his brother. Sometimes he came home only when the bars closed—drunk, hurting, unpredictable. And every day after, he still went to work. Meanwhile, I was left holding everything together with two small children.

One year, we experienced one of the largest earthquakes California had seen. Living on the second floor, I grabbed the kitchen table, pulled it away from the windows, and placed both babies underneath it. Jason was two and a half; Jessica was just born. I covered them with a blanket, praying the glass wouldn't shatter over them. It was my first true big earthquake—nothing like the little shakes I felt at my mom's house growing up. This time the entire building rocked and rattled. The pool water outside was splashing over the edges. It was terrifying.

I remember whispering, "Lord, protect us." I didn't know how to pray then, but that was enough.

When my husband came home later, it wasn't comforting. He laughed about how he stood on top of a shed at work "pretending to surf" during the earthquake. Meanwhile, my heart was still racing, trying to settle back into my chest.

And then came the drugs.

I am not blaming anyone for bringing them in. I allowed it. I participated. I opened the door that should have stayed shut forever. I exposed my children to an environment they never deserved. Yes, they were asleep or visiting friends or grandparents, but I still brought that darkness into our home. For that, I carry deep regret—and I owe an apology to myself... and to my daughter.

Jessica, I am sorry.

I'm sorry you grew up surrounded by pain, chaos, and brokenness. I'm sorry I wasn't the protector I should have been—for you or for your brother. The enemy took advantage of our ignorance. I didn't know better then. But I ask for your forgiveness.

What started off as "just a couple days" of using turned into every day. Crystal meth became crack cocaine. Our friends and relatives joined in. People supplied it. The house became a revolving door of addiction, and we survived on no sleep, no food, and no peace. We stayed up for hours—days sometimes—and still went to work.

Functioning addicts.

We thought we were fine. We thought we were hiding it. We weren't.

We wore sunglasses at the kids' sports games because the light hurt our eyes when we were crashing. Our skin was pale. Our bodies weak. Bags under our eyes. Sunken faces. Dehydrated. Sick. But we kept going—surviving, not living. Existing, not thriving. And we had no purpose. Our children were our only purpose, but we hadn't found our purpose in God yet.

Still, God's grace covered us—every mile we drove, every reckless decision we made. My husband drove drunk regularly. He drove our children while drunk. We bought drugs with them in the car.

We took risks we didn't even think about.

And as a mother, I was wrong. I can admit that.

Addiction sank its claws into us. During the moments we tried to stop, I went through withdrawals—headaches, exhaustion, no appetite, sleeping all day, unable to move. I started relying on getting high just to get out of bed. My morning "coffee" was methamphetamine to get me through work. At night, it was crack cocaine.

Alcohol wasn't my thing—just an occasional glass of wine. Drugs were my drug of choice. Even at birthday parties, we slipped inside, did a line or took a hit, then returned outside smiling, pretending everything was normal.

Until one night… everything changed.

I was scheduled to work a graveyard shift. But I never woke up. My body gave out. I finally woke around 11:10 PM—already late. I brushed my teeth, did a quick line, and rushed out the door. On the road, exhausted and drifting between lanes, I was pulled over. The officer asked if I was okay. I told him no—I had just woken up and was rushing to work. He checked my documents, delaying me further. I couldn't even call my job because we didn't have cell phones back then. He knew me from the hospital where he sometimes worked security and decided to follow me to ensure I arrived safely. He told the supervisor what happened. He even checked my pupils—he suspected I was under the influence but didn't say it outright.

The next day, I was let go.

They asked what was going on. I told them the truth: I was being abused. My husband had been calling my job constantly, checking on me, stalking me. He even shaved his beard and sat disguised at the bar where I worked as a cocktail waitress, hallucinating, thinking I was cheating. The drugs were destroying us both. The paranoia. The fighting. The chaos.

Soon, the conversation shifted to separation. Enough was enough. We started discussing what was best for the kids—but the truth is, we weren't thinking about the kids yet. We were thinking about ourselves. We both wanted the children. We both were broken. And we both were lost.

Chapter 5
Lost and Without Hope

We agreed to separate. He went to stay with his family, and I remained in the house with our children, still working as a cocktail waitress. Part-time hours weren't enough to cover rent or bills, so I applied for welfare and collected food stamps. Eventually, I gave up the job entirely to focus on raising my children. Even then, the three-bedroom house with the swimming pool was too expensive. I had to downsize to a two-bedroom apartment in Long Beach, California, one that was just barely affordable.

There I was, raising my kids alone. They rode the school bus to stay in the same classes with the same teachers, preserving some stability in their lives. My family helped me move, showing up with a Penske truck and loading everything we could into it. It was the beginning of a new chapter, but also the start of feeling truly lost.

At this point, I was fighting for custody of my children. Temporary joint custody allowed me to have them during the school week while their father had them on weekends, splitting holidays amicably. I had the support of my mother and stepfather, as well as my children's paternal grandparents. I credit them all for helping shape Jason and Jessica into the remarkable children they became. Without that network, I don't know how we would have survived.

Life settled into a fragile rhythm. The kids went to school, did homework, and participated in sports. I took Jason to his games and Jessica to hers, often juggling two parks at the same time. Their father and I remained cordial, and he sometimes came with his new girlfriend—who would later become his wife. But the depression had begun to creep in. I had lost everything I had worked for: the house, the stability, the life I thought I had built. Even though the house had held painful memories, it had also been filled with joy: family gatherings, birthday parties, sports celebrations, costumes, laughter. That world was gone.

I tried to fill the void with people. I went out to eat, to movies, to see different men—but it never worked. I was surviving, not living. Darkness was closing in.

One day, a friend from Lakewood appeared at my door. I had not seen her in six or seven months. She told me she was clean, and I let her in. We caught up, laughed a little, and then she asked if she could spend the night. I agreed. When I returned with the kids from school, she was sleeping. The next morning she left quietly, leaving me alone again—but she returned a week or two later. That time, she brought drugs.

At first, I hesitated. I had been clean, but I rationalized: "One time won't hurt." That one time became the worst mistake of my life. I smoked meth for the first time. The effects were immediate: itching, restlessness, obsession with cleaning, jumping from one task to another without finishing. I felt a twisted energy, a dangerous thrill.

That one encounter pulled me back into addiction. Occasionally, when the kids weren't home, I would get high with her or her friends. One man eventually became my boyfriend and moved in. At first, my children liked him; he seemed kind, helpful.

But my mother sensed something wrong, even if she couldn't explain it. Drugs returned, the addiction grew, and soon he began selling outside the apartment. One day, he came home in a panic: someone was after him with a gun. I had no choice but to take my kids to their father's house for safety and go on the run with him. We stayed in cheap hotels—Seal Beach, Long Beach—and I cleaned rooms or ran the front office in exchange for lodging. My boyfriend recycled appliances, doing hard labor to help us survive. Life was unstable, unsafe, and frightening, but at least we had a roof over our heads.

I reached a breaking point. Desperate to escape the despair of losing my children, I attempted suicide. I wrapped a telephone cord around my neck, but a maid walked in, called paramedics, and I was placed on a 72-hour mental health hold. After my release, I returned to the streets, with only the clothes I wore and what I could buy along the way. My shoes were worn through, my feet sore—but then I saw a woman in a wheelchair being pushed by her children. She had no legs, yet she radiated happiness. In that moment, I realized that even in my struggle, I had a reason to fight: my children. My desire to be with them, to rebuild, became my lifeline.

I began journaling my thoughts to regain control over my life. In a coloring book, I drew a merry-go-round and wrote, "It may seem like your life is going in circles, but it's up to you to get off. You have the power to stop it." On another page, an alligator lifted weights and sweated tears, with my words beside it: "In order to become strong, you must press through the opposition. You can't quit in the middle." These small reminders became my anchors.

I stayed connected to my children, calling them when they were with my mother or their other grandmother, mailing short letters to remind them I loved and missed them. It was a small hope—but it was enough to keep me moving forward.

Eventually, my boyfriend and I were offered on-site management positions at a run-down hotel in National City, San Diego. We were given a small apartment for free and tried to stabilize our lives. I even began college to become a phlebotomist, earning a loan and good grades. But the old temptations never left. Drugs were close, easily accessible from our neighbors. I dabbed again, and the addiction tugged at us relentlessly.

Our missteps cost us the apartment and our jobs. Two weeks to leave. Desperate, I called my mother for help. At first, she said no—but my stepfather intervened. With his encouragement, I went home, detoxing and slowly rebuilding. My kids visited on weekends, and I focused on sobriety. It was hard—very hard. Addiction leaves a deep scar, one that affects not just the user but everyone they love.

I had to piece myself back together, learn to forgive myself, and reclaim the life that had been stolen by poor choices. It was the hardest work I had ever done, but it was necessary. And I had to do it not just for me, but for my children, my family, and the life I wanted to live.

Chapter 6
Light at the End of the Tunnel

Moving back into my mother's house felt like walking backward in life. My head was low, my pride was bruised, and shame clung to me like a second skin. I felt small. Embarrassed. Weak. Depending on someone else felt like failure — but I didn't know then that stepping into her home would be the beginning of my healing, a slow walk back toward finding myself again.

Even though I had moved in, I was still struggling with addiction. I wasn't using as much, but I would still sneak out and do a line here, a line there — usually at a friend's house. When my kids came to visit me at my mom's place, I made sure those were my "clean days." I wouldn't use at all on the days they stayed with me. I wanted them to see the best parts of me, even though I felt so broken inside.

My mother laid down strict rules the moment I stepped through her door.

No smoking in the house.

A strict 10 p.m. curfew.

Doors locked.

No key for me.

And no cell phones back then — so if I wasn't home, she just waited, worried and helpless.

When I did stroll in at four or five in the morning, thinking it was no big deal, she would confront me:

"I was up all night. Every siren, every helicopter — I thought it was you. I thought something happened."

I hadn't even considered her fear. I was too wrapped up in my own world — a world of late-night computer games, friends' living rooms, lines of drugs, and a false sense of freedom. Meanwhile, she was at home praying I didn't end up dead.
Eventually her patience wore thin. She was tired of me laying around, sleeping all day, doing nothing. She challenged me to get a job — and something in me knew she was right.

Back when job hunting meant flipping through newspaper ads, I highlighted openings, made calls, lined up interviews. My stepfather — a gentle, kind man who had become the father I never had — drove me to every interview. To this day, I thank God I had him in my life.
My first seasonal job was at a famous chocolate factory during Christmas.
I packed and wrapped orders, handing boxes to customers with a smile I barely felt. At the same time, I worked nights at a major toy warehouse, stocking shelves and unloading conveyor belts. I used drugs to stay awake — or at least that's what I told myself. The truth was, my body didn't know how to function without it anymore.
But even in my addiction, work gave me something I hadn't felt in a long time: hope.
Just a glimmer.
Just enough light to see the possibility of a future.
The seasonal jobs didn't provide stability, though. I knew I needed something better — something consistent if I ever wanted to rebuild my life or earn back the right to be a full-time mother.

Eventually, I found a regular job at a motorcycle shop. I answered phones, pulled parts, helped customers. Sometimes we had company outings at the lake — racing Sea-Doos, barbecuing, enjoying a taste of normal life. I brought my kids with me, and for the first time, I was trusted to be with them without supervision. My heart soaked in every minute.

With time, I met someone — a man I had gone to school with. We started dating, and he ended up being good to me. Respectful. Sober. Stable. My mom and stepfather liked him, and my children grew comfortable around him. We eventually got engaged and bought a house in Corona, California. For the first time in a very long time, it looked like my life was finally turning around.

But life isn't always a straight path. And my past had a way of following me.

When we moved to Corona, I couldn't keep my job in Bellflower. I needed something local. Desperate for work, I answered a vague ad — and ended up working as a tarot card reader. It wasn't what I expected, but it paid the bills. And even though I wasn't saved yet, something strange happened during those calls. I found myself encouraging people, speaking hope into them, talking about healing and purpose. People would call back just to speak to me again.

I didn't realize it then, but God was using me long before I knew Him.

But my life began unraveling again when my teenage daughter became pregnant. She was only 13, and the father — a boy who lied about his age — was 19. It turned into a legal mess. CPS got involved. Her father tried to take her from me. But I refused to let history repeat itself. I fought for her. I fought for that baby. I fought because deep down, I knew I couldn't lose my daughter.

Then we lost the house.

We had nowhere to go. We ended up staying in Tecate, Mexico with the baby's father's family before the baby was born. While she was there, I bounced in and out of the streets — homeless, lost, surviving however I could. I slept in friends' yards, in tents, wherever I could find space.

I asked my mom to pick me up once, desperate and broken. She told me:

"No. You're never going to change."

That broke something inside me.

In desperation, I got involved in transporting drugs — thinking it was just "one run" so I could get a car and some money. I had no idea I was a decoy for something much bigger. When the dogs sniffed out 80 pounds of marijuana hidden in the wheels and fenders, I was arrested.

I spent 30 days in county jail — and during that time, my granddaughter was born.

Once I was released, I had no home to go to. No car. No plan. And the only person who offered to pick me up was a man connected to one of my cellmate's "boyfriends" — who turned out to be a pimp.

And just like that, I found myself on the streets of San Diego watching girls get sent out on "the track." Some had beepers for clients, some had quotas, all had fear. I was being trained. They were preparing to send me out next.

But God stepped in.

Before my first "date," something in me snapped. I ran. I hitchhiked out of San Diego and ended up back in Riverside County. The man who gave me a ride bought me a meal, listened to my story, and dropped me off safely. That was nothing but God's grace.

Back in Corona, I stayed in half-built houses — squatting. No heat, no plumbing, no blankets. Just a body, a floor, and a drug addiction that wouldn't let me go. To survive, I sold drugs. I rented cheap motel rooms with whatever money I could scrape together. And yet, through it all, I kept having these quiet moments with God.

Moments where I would whisper, "Lord, I'm hungry,"
and someone would show up with food.
Moments where I just needed a safe place to nap,
and suddenly a couch would appear.
I didn't know how to pray — but somehow, He heard me anyway.
When the people in my drug circle were raided, and I barely escaped
being caught with them, I knew my time was running out. I hitchhiked
again, trying to reach the desert where my son lived — but instead,
another pimp caught me and dragged me into Los Angeles.
This time, there was no "training."
No warnings.
No excuses.
They put me straight out on the street.
And the rules were simple:
Bring back money.
Or get beaten.
In front of everyone.
Their "empire," they called it.
And that's where this chapter ends — in a place darker than I had ever
imagined, yet somehow, even then, God was still holding onto me.

Chapter 7
Surrendering

He told me to be careful as I stepped out, but in my mind, I had already made my decision:
I wasn't coming back to that hotel room.
They had booked their flights and made it clear we needed to be back by checkout because they were heading for the airport—and I was expected to go with them. But the moment I walked out that door with my little purse and my jail ID, I knew I was leaving for good. I didn't know where I was going, but I knew I wasn't going back.

I ended up at a regular city bus stop, trying to look like I had a plan, even though I didn't. Another pimp approached me, but before he could pull me in, I hopped into my first trick car with a plan of survival. I told the man straight up, "Take me as far down the Strip as you can. Just drop me off. I'm running away from a pimp."

By then, I could recognize a pimp instantly—the tone, the cars, the language, the girls, the signals. I understood sex trafficking, and I knew the danger I was in. These men carried guns. This wasn't some careless situation—this was captivity.
In the back of my mind I kept praying, Lord, if I could ever get out of this alive, please protect me. That prayer stayed with me whether I was sober or high.
The man drove me to a hotel parking garage where we sat for about an hour. I cried the entire time. He didn't try anything—he just talked to me, fed me, and told me, "You've got to have faith. You're going to be okay." His kindness stunned me. Eventually he drove me down to a rough neighborhood called Naked City and dropped me off.

I felt safer only because I knew the pimps worked the other end of the Strip. But I was still lost, still scared, still wandering. Eventually I found people—because addicts can always identify each other. I got high again. I started selling again. I did whatever I had to do to get a $20–$25 room or a safe couch.

A security guard let me sleep in a vacant apartment for $20 a night as long as I was out by 6 a.m. I learned survival without relying on anyone. I even sent postcards home to my kids pretending everything was fine. I stayed on couches, in abandoned places, and mostly with drug dealers. I became the runner—taking drugs out to the cars, bringing money back. I even met the cook. I was making more money than ever, but I was getting busted constantly for possession and paraphernalia. Each time they released me, I went right back to the streets.

I remember once sitting on the steps of a church, hoping—praying—that someone inside would help me. When the usher opened the door, he told me, "You need to move. You don't belong here. We're getting ready to open."

"I'm here for help," I said, but he didn't care.
He told me again to leave.
The way that crushed me... I felt like a leper—unclean, unwanted, unworthy. If God could turn His face from me too, then who was left? I tried taking my life again. Multiple overdoses. Exhaustion. Despair. One day, a woman I got high with left to "re-up." I stayed behind. She shot up with heroin cut with battery acid. They found her in an alley, foaming at the mouth, needle still in her arm. That was supposed to be me.

The next day, another man tried to get me to inject crack mixed with heroin. I had the band on my arm, the needle about to touch my vein—and something came over me. I shoved his hand away and tore off the tourniquet.

God spared me both days, even when I didn't want to be spared. One day in the alley, an officer approached—Officer Dow. She didn't come at me with authority; she came with compassion. "I just want to talk to you," she'd say. And every day she tried. Every day I avoided her. Yet she persisted.

She said, "You don't belong out here. You deserve better." Her words ministered to me deeper than she ever knew. The church told me I didn't belong there.

But an officer told me I didn't belong on the streets.
Years later, I understood why God placed her in my life. She watered seeds I didn't even know existed. To this day, we co-labor in ministry. God used her to help save my life.

Still, during that time, I felt lost. My mom wouldn't accept my collect calls. She rejected every one. The only person who ever picked up was my mother-in-law. She wrote letters filled with Scriptures. She prayed for me. She reminded me that God would never leave me nor forsake me.

But I felt forsaken. I felt trapped between my past and my pain. Sober for a couple of days in jail, reality hit hard. What am I doing with my life? How did I get here?

My plan was simple: buy enough crack to kill myself.

I even checked myself into a mental ward to overdose on depression meds. When that didn't work, I went right back to the streets with the same intention.

Then one day, a man approached me in the alley.
"What are you doing out here?" he asked.
"Nothing," I said.
"Are you hungry?"
No one had asked me that in so long. I realized how little I'd eaten. He took me inside, fed me a sandwich, and then asked, "Will you come back tomorrow at 6 p.m.? I want to make you a real meal."
I left feeling something I hadn't felt in a long time:
hope.
The next day I returned.

When I walked in, the man was playing a keyboard, singing about being "washed in the blood of the Lamb." I didn't understand any of it. He opened his Bible and began teaching from John 3:16.
As he spoke, something pierced through the fog of addiction.
I remembered saying the sinner's prayer at nine years old with the little girl across the street. The same words. The same feeling. The same peace.
He asked me, "What are you doing out here? Why are you on these streets?"

His words echoed Officer Dow's. God was speaking through strangers, watering seeds the church had rejected.
He told me to go to a church nearby and wrote me a blank check. "I'm sowing into you," he said. "You have a choice. You can cash it for yourself… or you can walk into that sanctuary and let God change your life."
And right there, God was calling me to surrender.

I still have that letter.
Her words crushed me. I had gone into that home hoping she would finally be proud of me—hoping she would see that I was trying, that I wanted help. All I ever wanted was her approval. But instead, old echoes filled my mind: You'll never succeed. You'll never change. You'll always be the same old Sharon.
Those weren't just thoughts—they were wounds. Wounds the enemy loved to reopen.
Being denied as her child pulled me into an even deeper place of grief. I wasn't just grieving my family. I was grieving myself. My identity. My sense of worth. Who I thought I was, and who I feared I would never become.

Learning to Face Myself

At the home, they talked a lot about "taking off the masks." Looking at the real you. I didn't know how to do that. When the other women would joke around, even playfully, I didn't know how to take it. I folded inward. There were days I would curl up in a corner, feeling exposed, raw, and out of place.

They were full of joy and full of the Lord.
I felt cut open and bleeding on the inside—yet invisible.
That pain became a major part of my recovery. Healing wasn't just about getting off drugs. It was healing my emotions, my mind, my soul—being delivered from everything that had attached itself to me long before addiction ever entered the picture.

Chapter 8
Grief and Loss

They dropped me off at the Christian Recovery Women's Home, and the weight of everything I was carrying settled into my chest. Before I surrendered myself to the rules of the program, I wanted to call my mother—to let her know I was safe and where I was staying. I had rarely called her before. Most times she wouldn't answer, or the call would go straight to the machine. And even if I left a message, she never returned the call. She monitored everything.

But that day, I just wanted her to know where I was. For the first two weeks in the program, there was no outside contact at all—no calls, no letters, no visits. It was a time of consecration, meant to disconnect you from the world and force your focus toward God and your future.

The staff gave me permission to make one phone call. I dialed, expecting the usual silence. But this time she answered. Her voice was hesitant, almost suspicious, like she was waiting for me to ask for something. I told her where I was and that I was safe.

Her reaction was not what I hoped for. When she heard I was in a Christian recovery home, she became upset. My mother is Jewish, and she didn't understand why I didn't choose a Jewish rehab. "If you would have just asked me," she said sharply, "I would've helped you find one. There are plenty in your area."

We ended the call on cold, unfamiliar ground.

Weeks later, when I was finally allowed to receive mail, I got a letter from her—a letter that pierced me deeper than anything I'd experienced in my addiction. She wrote that she was a Jewish mother with three Jewish children, but that one had decided to go astray… and that when she died, only two of her children would be welcome at her funeral.

Entering Into Prayer

Life in the home was structured. Strict. They woke us at 4:30 a.m., and by 5:00 we were in the sanctuary. I didn't know how to pray. All I could say was, "Dear God, help me. Lord, help me."

During prayer time, I would listen to the other women and quietly say, "Yes, God… what she said." If someone prayed to see her kids again, I whispered, "Me too." If someone prayed for a job, I said, "Me too, God."

Little by little, I learned to talk to Him for myself.

I learned that He listens.

And I learned that I could ask for more than survival—I could ask to know Him.

One day I prayed, "I've heard about You, but I want to know You for myself."

Those words changed everything.

God began to reveal Himself—not in a loud voice, but in memories. In moments He brought back to my mind:

When I was a child with no father—He had been my Father.

When I was in the streets—He protected me even when I didn't want protection.

When I was lost—He had already set me apart.

He showed me He had never left me.
Christianity stopped being a "religion." It became a relationship.
A relationship with a God who loved me even when I didn't love myself.

Redefining My Life

As I learned His character—His love, His forgiveness—I learned to extend those things to others… and to myself. For the first time, I began forgiving myself for the choices I made that hurt my family, my kids, and even myself.

In my mind, I pictured recovery as simple:

Get clean. Get a job. Get my kids. Live happily ever after.

But real life required a process. Courts. Schools. Stability. Time.

And trust.

And though I didn't know it yet, the path God had for me would be nothing like the one I imagined. He was about to lead me into one of the most life-altering seasons I would ever walk through.

A Pain That Revealed a Deeper Battle

People at the home noticed I was walking strangely. I kept losing my balance. One morning, getting dressed for church, I collapsed again—this time spraining my ankle. At the ER, the doctors weren't just concerned about the sprain. They saw something else. Something deeper. Reflexes weren't responding. Tests came back abnormal. They asked about family history. They prepared for a spinal tap.

Then came the scan that changed my life:

A tumor the size of a softball wrapped around my spinal cord.

It was crushing the nerves.

It was slowly paralyzing me.

And it was growing.

They called a neurosurgeon immediately.

Drugged and terrified, I signed for emergency surgery. My mother was contacted. The home director and a pastor came to pray over me.

They told me there was a high chance I would wake up permanently paralyzed.

At that point, I just wanted the pain to stop.

Paralyzed

The surgery was eight hours. They had to cut through my spinal cord to remove the tumor and then reconstruct everything with bone and metal.

When I woke up, I couldn't move anything from the waist down.

Not a toe.

Not a foot.

Not a leg.

It felt like another body was lying on top of me. Heavy. Dead.

I was paralyzed.

And yet my first prayer was:

"God, even if I never walk again… let me still be a woman who can pray on her knees."

But even kneeling was impossible.
They told me I would need months in the hospital—first in acute care, then in an intensive rehabilitation center. The women from the home visited once or twice, but life went on for them. I was alone.
Except for one woman—Rachel Richardson. She came faithfully, prayed with me, encouraged me. Her visits were a lifeline.

Learning to Live Again

For months, therapists worked to restore circulation, prevent blood clots, and strengthen what muscles were left. They taught me how to transfer myself from bed to wheelchair, how to use my arms for mobility, and how to regain independence piece by piece.
I learned how to use a commode.
How to brush my teeth again without help.
How to grab items with a reacher.
How to pull pants on with the "frog-leg" method.
How to stand for 30 seconds—then a minute—then ten.
Worship got me through those days. I had a little CD player, and I would sit in my wheelchair with headphones on, singing until tears came. I couldn't lift my arms high, but I lifted my heart.
And in that place of helplessness, God taught me gratitude.
"Thank You for breath in my lungs."
"Thank You for my eyes."
"Thank You that my legs are still attached."
He reminded me of the woman I once saw with no legs when I was homeless.
He showed me that even in my paralysis—I was blessed.

Five Years of Battles, Miracles, and Lessons

I eventually moved into a transitional living wing where I could live independently with limited aid. I learned to walk again—first with a walker, then with a cane. Progress was slow and painful.

Five years after the first surgery, I had to undergo another one. The top of my spine was closing off. They opened me from the base of my skull downward and stabilized my neck with screws and metal. Recovery started all over again.

But I walked.
Not perfectly.
Not quickly.
But I walked.

Surrendering My Plans

The biggest lesson came when I realized that everything I planned in the beginning—the dreams of immediately getting my kids back, the picture of a perfect restored life—was not God's plan.

His plan was bigger.
His plan was different.
His plan required surrender.

I entered the recovery home wanting to fix my life.
God brought me there to transform my life.
He wasn't preparing me to simply go back to who I was.
He was preparing me for who He called me to be.

Chapter 9
Just Existing but Not Really Living

Rachel Richardson—the woman who faithfully visited me—was the one who first took me back to church. She came to the facility, picked me up, loaded my wheelchair, and sat with me through the entire service. The doctors had approved what they called a "pass," meaning I could leave for a short time as long as someone would watch over me and transport me safely. I had to be medically cleared, proving I was strong enough to be out for an hour and a half without risk.

Rachel's willingness to take me in my wheelchair was a blessing I will never forget. I still remember how the Word felt that day—alive, refreshing, healing. When I returned to the facility, I was overflowing with joy simply because I was outside. Because I was reminded that I still had life. Because I was reminded that God had not forgotten me.

The facility was filled with elderly residents. People were dying around me. It felt like a waiting room for a senior home, and I was decades younger than everyone else. Being in my forties, wheelchair-bound, in a place like that—it was surreal. Yet something inside me refused to die there.
I would roll through those halls singing. Worship poured out of me. One day a lady stopped me and asked, almost confused,

"Why are you so happy? You're in a wheelchair. You're stuck here. This place is awful."
I smiled and said,
"I'm happy because I have life—and God has given me a second chance."
People began watching me, but what they were really seeing was the joy of the Lord carrying me through my pain. That became my ministry in that place—not through sermons or long conversations, but through the way I praised God in my condition. When people see you worship through what should've destroyed you, that's when your witness becomes the loudest.

Soon residents were asking me to pray for them. I would roll my wheelchair right into their rooms and pray, sing, or read the Word with them. There was one woman in particular who couldn't speak. She wrote on a tablet asking for prayer to get her voice back. We prayed together often. Eventually she was taken to the hospital for surgery, and when she returned, her voice had been restored. A massive blood clot had been blocking her throat. She stood in front of me with her healing testimony, and I rejoiced—not because of me, but because God would still use me even when I felt I had nothing left.

I had only my heart and my voice to give Him, and that was enough.
Her story stayed with me. She had been broadsided by a motorcycle—its chain system slicing through the car like a saw and into her face and throat. She had undergone reconstruction and complex surgeries. Yet God allowed me to speak into her life, to pray with her, to remind her that even when the enemy comes to kill, steal, and destroy, God still has the final say.
And He was using me—broken, healing, learning to walk again—to minister His love to her.

Released to Live on My Own

Eventually the doctors agreed I was ready to live independently. Through Medicaid, the state offered vouchers that paid for a small apartment—actually an old hotel converted into living units. It wasn't much, but it was mine.

I was still learning to walk, to cook, to manage on my own again. I didn't stay long, though. I eventually moved in with my former pastors—the couple I had served under when I was the women's home director. Because everything was approved, the voucher was transferred to them. Before moving in with them, I stayed in other voucher-approved places, but what happened during this season of my life is what stands out the most.

One day we all went out to eat at a buffet—my pastor, his wife, and me. As we sat there, the Lord spoke so clearly to my spirit:

"Get rid of your wheelchair."

Immediately I recognized it as Scripture—"Take up your mat and walk."

My wheelchair was my mat. It was what I leaned on. It was my safety, my comfort, my crutch. God was challenging me: Give it up. Trust Me.

I looked across the restaurant and saw an older man sitting with his daughter. His wheelchair was old, heavy, and bulky. I approached him and said gently,

"Sir, would you like a new wheelchair?"

He looked confused. "Why?"

I explained that mine was custom-made—lightweight, quick-release wheels, air cushion, specialized seating for my spinal injury. It folded easily and was designed specifically to protect the fragile condition of my spine.

His daughter immediately said yes—they had been struggling with the heavy chair. We exchanged information and made arrangements for them to pick it up.

My pastor asked, "Why did you give your wheelchair away?"

I didn't tell him the whole truth. Some instructions from God are too precious to expose.

"I just don't need it anymore," I said.

And slowly—obedient step by obedient step—healing began to manifest. I regained strength. I walked more. I returned to part-time work—just eleven hours a week since Medicaid limited how much income I could make. I took three buses to work. I went from paratransit wheelchair transportation to climbing the bus steps by holding the railings, one slow step at a time.

I loved working. I loved church. I loved feeling alive again.

A Boss Who Saw My Potential

My boss at the time—Stephen Deutsch, who gave me permission to use his name—saw something in me I didn't even see in myself. He recognized my drive, my heart for people, and the way I treated customers with compassion and patience. I wasn't working for money. I was working from purpose.

People often told me they felt peace around me, and I truly believe it was God shining through. If someone needed prayer, I prayed. If someone needed encouragement, I offered it. Many asked if I was a Christian, and some I invited to church.

Stephen kept pushing me to grow. He believed in me. Because of him, I became a "floater," working at multiple locations. It was still part-time, but I began working so many hours that I earned more than Medicaid allowed. I eventually lost my Medicaid and my free medical care, but honestly, I was proud. I felt independent for the first time in years.

Stephen continued to encourage me, recommend me, and speak highly of me. We remained close friends for years.

The Loss of My Son

This part of my story is painful, and even now, my heart tightens as I revisit it.

I was at lunch with a friend from work, scrolling through Facebook, when I saw a picture of a white Mustang crushed against a mountainside—hood ripped open, windshield shattered, seat pushed back unnaturally far. The caption said the highway was backed up from a single-car accident and the driver was in critical condition. As a prayer warrior, I immediately prayed for whoever was inside that car.

But a fear rose up in me—That looks like my son's car.

I prayed harder, pleading with God that it wasn't him. I shared the post, asking others to pray.

Then came a comment:

"That is your son."

My breath left my body.

I started calling everyone—my son, my daughter, my daughter-in-law—anyone who might know where he was. Finally, his sister answered. He was in the hospital. They didn't think he would make it.

My entire world stopped.

He lived in California. I was in Las Vegas. I had recently relearned how to drive and obtained my license, but I didn't own a car. With urgency and desperation, I rented one. My boss told me, "Take all the time you need," and I left everything behind—job, rent, responsibilities.

On the drive, I sang the same worship song over and over:

"You deserve the glory… You do miracles so great."

I was completely enveloped in God's presence. I couldn't even feel the road beneath me. My only prayer was,

"God, save my son. Let his soul be Yours."

When I finally reached California, I prayed over him with anointing oil. Pastors came to pray as well. His injuries were severe—he had hydroplaned on a rainy road, overcorrected, and hit the mountain. He was thrown through the back windshield, his head striking the concrete divider. His brain had stroked out, only a small portion of the brain stem functioning.

Doctors warned us not to touch him due to sensory response concerns, but during prayer, I gently placed my hand on his shoulder. As I prayed, a tear slid down his cheek, and he let out a small moan.

I believe with everything in me that Jesus touched him in that moment. But the medical team told us this was as far as he would recover. He had previously told his wife he never wanted to remain on life support. The decision was heartbreaking, but it honored his wishes.

I returned to Vegas the next morning and went straight to church. They prayed for me, comforted me… but as I stepped into the foyer afterward, a leader approached me and said something that pierced me to my core: "All of this—your paralysis, your son's condition—is because of your rebellion and disobedience."

That was the enemy speaking through her.

Anger and divine fire rose up inside me. I went straight to the senior pastor and told him exactly what was said—and that I would no longer be attending his church. For ten years, I had given everything to that ministry. I had served faithfully, joyfully, wholeheartedly. And in my darkest season, this was the leadership's response.

I left devastated, wounded, and deeply disappointed.

And now, living alone, working more hours, and holding onto an apartment I could barely afford, I found myself asking God…

Chapter 10
Finding My Purpose

I found myself doing what came naturally—talking to people, giving out resources, evangelizing, inviting folks to church or my community group, pointing them toward food pantries, and helping wherever I could. If someone needed diapers, toiletries, or anything essential, I would go get it. Serving became a lifeline for me. It was my way of giving back while I was still trying to heal.

On Mother's Day, I started a small outreach of my own. I would buy roses, candy, sometimes little pieces of jewelry, and gather a few of my friends. We walked the streets where homeless women and prostitutes stayed, handing out gifts simply to remind them that they were loved. I ministered to them the best way I knew how—with compassion.

I'll never forget one particular woman who asked, "Why are you doing this?" She looked so broken. I told her honestly, "God told me to give this to you." She collapsed into tears. She had just lost her mother on Mother's Day. God used me, in my own grieving, to restore a little bit of faith in hers.

Even with all this serving, I still felt like I hadn't found my true purpose. I wasn't in "ministry" yet, at least not in the traditional sense. But looking back, God had already given me my own ministry—right where I was. I would go to Lorenzi Park with bags of McDonald's and Little Debbies, feeding the homeless and praying for people. I didn't have a title, but I had a heart that was willing.

Still, I kept praying, "Lord, what is my purpose? What did You call me to do?" Jeremiah 29 reminded me that God already knew the plans He had for my life. He had predestined, called, and chosen me long before I was tired of always being the strong one, the encourager, the one reigniting faith in others. I wanted someone who could pour back into me.

There were moments when even the women in the home came to me saying, "Sister Sharon, I'm going through it." And I would smile and say, "Praise God." They'd look confused, but I reminded them, "If you're going through something, that means a blessing is coming." I spoke hope into them—words that I later had to swallow myself. But still... something was missing. I didn't yet feel like I was doing what God ultimately called me to do.

One day, at a community event in Las Vegas where I was praying with the homeless and inviting people to church, I noticed a group wearing black polo shirts that said "Chaplain." They were out there with police officers on a RECAP call—Restore Every Community Around Peace—supporting families after homicides or suicides. They weren't just providing resources; they were praying, evangelizing, comforting.

I remember thinking, This is what I already do... just with a uniform. I asked questions, learned about the ministry, and eventually connected with Messages of Faith Ministries—Chaplaincy Nevada. I signed up, submitted my application, and in 2016, I officially became a chaplain. My very first shadow call was heartbreaking. A police officer in our community had been killed in a wrong-way crash while on duty. I wasn't even in uniform yet, but there I was—praying with grieving family members, holding a mother whose son was never coming home.
In that moment, something clicked in my spirit.
This is it.
To sit with someone in their pain, to hold them through their grief, to be a vessel of God's love in the darkest moments—that felt like purpose.
I continued to shadow and train through 2016, not knowing that 2017 would change my life forever.
Then came October 1st.

It was an all-hands-on-deck call. Chaplains were assigned all over the city—hospitals, the Strip, Metro headquarters. I was stationed at Metro with family members waiting for news about their loved ones from the Route 91 shooting. I hadn't even turned on the news; the Holy Spirit simply woke me and told me to go.

People arrived covered in blood—clothes, faces, everything. It looked unreal, like a movie scene, except it was real life.

One man sat alone, rocking back and forth, trembling. No chaplain was with him. I walked over, gently touched his hand, and said, "Sir, my name is Chaplain Sharon. May I pray with you?"

He broke completely. His sister had been at the concert, and no one could reach her. I prayed over him—for peace, for protection, for God to intervene. We sat together for hours, mostly in silence, waiting for names that felt like they would never be called.

Finally, a call came. His sister was alive. She had hidden under the stage until it was safe. We both cried and held each other. To this day, we're still friends, and every October 1st, I send him a message letting him know I'm praying for him.

The next day, at the Convention Center, we were assigned to families receiving the personal belongings of those who had died. Phones. Wallets. Wedding rings. We offered comfort in whatever way was appropriate—Christian, Muslim, Buddhist, or simply silent presence. It wasn't the moment to preach; it was the moment to hold broken hearts.

That was the beginning of my deep relationship with Chaplaincy Nevada.

As I grew, God expanded my ministry. I became a mentor with Hope for Prisoners under John Ponder and eventually became a case manager. I supported people dealing with anger, substance abuse, broken families, and the struggle to rebuild their lives.

. Discipleship was natural to me. Helping women heal and grow felt like home.
But eventually, due to nerve damage and neurological issues, I had to leave my full-time position. That loss was painful in its own way. Still, Hope for Prisoners remains family. I cover them in prayer, and they know I'm just a phone call away.

I also joined the Adopt-a-Cop program, praying for officers, firefighters, EMTs, veterans, and their families. My husband and I even adopted the family of a fallen officer one Christmas, bringing gifts and meals to honor the father who wasn't there.
Another ministry God opened was spiritual recovery in the women and children's shelter—teaching biblical principles through a twelve-step format to prepare women for reentry into the community.
Throughout all of this—ministry, serving, chaplaincy—I kept praying for my husband. I dated a few men here and there, but God always showed me red flags. Months would go by with no one but me and God. I stayed celibate for twenty years, even through depression, grief, and loneliness. God carried me.

He was preparing me.
Preparing my purpose.
Preparing my heart.
Preparing my future.

MY NOTES

MY NOTES

MY NOTES

MY NOTES

MY NOTES

MY NOTES

MY NOTES

MY NOTES

MY NOTES

MY NOTES

MY NOTES

MY NOTES

MY NOTES

MY NOTES

MY NOTES

MY NOTES

MY NOTES

MY NOTES

MY NOTES

MY NOTES

MY NOTES

MY NOTES

MY NOTES

MY NOTES

MY NOTES

Made in the USA
Coppell, TX
17 January 2026

65644937R10049